where blessings flow

WORDS OF GLORY AND THANKS

Anna Burke

VERITAS

First published 2007 by
Veritas Publications
7/8 Lower Abbey Street
Dublin 1
Ireland

Email publications@veritas.ie
Website www.veritas.ie

ISBN 978 1 84730 046 1

Scripture passages adapted from the *Christian Community Bible*,
Catholic Pastoral Edition, courtesy of Claretian Publications, 2004.

A catalogue record for this book is available from the British
Library.

Printed in the Republic of Ireland by Betaprint Ltd, Dublin

Veritas books are printed on paper made from the wood pulp of
managed forests. For every tree felled, at least one tree is planted,
thereby renewing natural resources.

I dedicate this book to all the men, women and children who search for blessings amid the rubble and emptiness of poverty. Against all the odds these are the people who hold tenderly a sense of God as they search for bread and water. This little book is for them.

CONTENTS

INTRODUCTION

The Touch of God

As he blessed them he withdrew.

Luke 24:50

The farewell action of Christ on earth is his blessing on the Church. In this final gesture he is sealing his relationship with us, for ever. In the giving and in the receiving of the blessing there is the shared participation in the abundance of God's generosity and in the faithful movement of God's breath through the timeless story.

To bless someone is to offer a most special gift. The words and the gestures used in this sacred communication trace all gift – giving back to God. Every blessing has its origin in the touch of God and when we bless we connect the moment of encounter to the holy well.

In the biblical tradition blessings are symbolised with water, which in itself throbs with life-giving. This indispensable element awakens in us a thirst for the living spring and the water beckons us to immerse ourselves in the gifts that God is offering. We use holy water in our social greetings, in our liturgical ritual, in prayer at mealtime and as protection for the journey to connect the moments of every day to the source of life.

The blessing recognises the existence of God, from whom all blessings flow. When we bless we ask and give, we receive and bestow, the touch of God.

CHAPTER ONE

The Blessing of Springtime,
of a Birthday, of the Meadow,
of the Bog

THE BLESSING OF SPRINGTIME

*Come then, my love; my lovely one,
come with me.
The winter is over; the rains have stopped;
In the countryside the flowers are in bloom.
This is the time for singing.*

Song of Songs 2:10-12

Springtime Thoughts

O God, you call me from the sleep of Winter, to shake off the dead leaves of yesterday's slumber and to awaken again to awareness and to light. As the ice cap recedes from my horizon, the tomb of my senses begins to open and I breathe again the smell of life, into my spirit, into all my feelings. I have learned from the silent time. It held my life in strong hands until my waiting time was over and I was able to emerge again into the sunlight of my dream. My voice is stronger now and I find my melody in the dawn chorus.

I have learned from the silent time. Deep down in the cave of sleep I heard the sound of growing pains. It played in waves against my senses and it beat against my withdrawal. The sound grew and resounded until the cave became the orchestral chamber and my slumbering muscles got caught up in the rhythm. My spirit groaned in the moment of rebirth and my body felt her courage. I have learned from the silent time. The moon is nearer now and I can touch the stillness of her face. The stars are forming new shapes and I can catch their golden particles in my eyes, opening me to wonder. I am reborn as Spring, soft again, delicate again, fertile again. The snowdrop is restoring the hope of man and beast and the frost is melting for the new grass. The whole of nature is changing her colour and the pores of the earth are giving out a living scent.

It is springtime in my heart and in my thoughts. I have come through the frozen time and I see now the movement in the shadows.

— I Bless You —

I bless your awakening today. May the opening of your eyes be gentle with expectation.

I bless you with the softness of the moistened earth. May the molecules of soil part for your passing through.

I bless you with the pure kiss of the snowdrop. May it give you courage and hope as you face the wind and the rain.

I bless you with the early bud, holding the possibility. May it be in you a belief in little steps and in life visions.

I bless you with the opening seed, revealing the secret of life. May it burst open in your heart and call you forth to flowering.

I bless you with the song of the bird, announcing the nesting season. May it call you to the melody of life and love.

I bless you with the colour of the cherry blossom, fragile in the breeze. May it reveal to you the many colours in everything.

I bless you with the dance of the daffodil, waltzing in the garden. May it lead you in the dance.

THE BLESSING OF A BIRTHDAY

*Before you were conceived in the womb
I knew you.*

Psalms 139

Birthday Thoughts

In the beginning the breath of God moved over the empty space and there was a stirring in the cosmic dust. Life came forth from the holy breath and a godly expression began to be seen. The perspective grew and deepened and reached its divine intensity when the man and the woman walked forth from the Breath. They had the heart of the artist and they were capable of thinking and of feeling like God.

In the beginning God imagined you. You would be unique in the chain of life, with a great heart and with a special touch. You would have possibility to scale the heights and to paint new colours. You would do it in your own time and at your own pace and in your own way. As God imagined the web of relationships that weave the sacred unity of life, you came into being. On the 'fifth' day of the 'seventh' month of the year '2007' in the third millennium of the Christian era, you entered the creation story. It was 'seven' minutes 'after midnight.' The angels sang at your birth and the stars sprayed sparkles of gold in the heavens. There was joy beyond measure in the family and in the neighbourhood and friends came to see you, offering gifts and words of blessing.

The day of your birth is written into history now and it is written into our lifeline. It is a day about love and about miracles and about wonder and about gratitude.

The one we have waited for is with us. We welcome you as God welcomes you.

We will walk the road beside you when you are slow and when you are fast, when you are weak and when you are strong; for you are our sacred thrust and we love you as God loves you.

Happy Birthday!

— I Bless You —

May the blessing of life fill your days with
energy and with joy.

May the blessing of your birth awaken in you
a thirst for beginning things.

May the blessing of your tiny fingers give you
the imagination of an artist and the skill of a
designer.

May the blessing of your hands give you a
desire to reach beyond the limits.

May the blessing of your smile be a light on
the pages of your story.

May the blessing of your mind fill you with
wisdom and with insight.

May the blessing of your heart give you the
freedom of the seagull until you find your still
point.

May the blessing of your body be a channel of
good health and good experience.

May the blessing of your family guide your
search for love, for God.

May the blessing of your faith-community
nurture your talents and your inspiration.

May the blessing of your name open your ears
to hear the voice of life and destiny.

The Blessing of the Meadow

*It is God who clothes the wild grass —
grass that is here today and gone
tomorrow, burnt up in the oven. Will he
not be all the more sure to clothe you?*

Luke 12:27-28

Meadow Thoughts

I picked up the milk today! It was fresh and
fridge-cold and it poured over my porridge with
the richness of life-giving things. As I relaxed
over breakfast I gazed at the cows in the
meadow beyond the kitchen window. On that
first spoonful I thanked God for them and for
their gift of milk that sustains the life in us, and
for the farmer who nourishes the cows and milk
them every day, twice a day. I also mentioned
the early morning vans that get the milk to the
shops and the drivers who never get a sleep-in.
Then I remembered the people in the creamery

who prepare the milk for distribution. I was still on my first spoonful when the thought of shopkeepers came to me, especially the ones who receive the van drivers and stack the cartons for the customers. This was my prayer at breakfast. God had truly clothed me in a thankful moment.

As I blessed the meadow for her early morning meditation I took the children to school in the old banger. It is all of fifteen years on the road and it still safeguarded the family banter, the arguments and the laughter. As we waited at the traffic lights, I went back to the thought of the meadow and reliable things and reliable people. I recalled that this old car was made in Germany and that a chain of people brought it to my family. These were good people and responsible people and skilled people. They had used their gifts of time and talent to bring to birth, to perfect and to serve. I remembered them all in my prayer at the traffic lights. God had truly clothed me with the blessing of the meadow.

— I Bless You —

I bless you in your growing time over many miles and years. May it show you the wisdom of rooting deep within.

I bless you in your playing time through fields of wild flowers. May it give you on your journey a scent for life.

I bless you in your dancing time on the arms of the wind. May it lead you stepping softly to the rhythm of the grasses.

I bless you in your joyful time of laughter and of song. May it weave for your achievement a garland of daisies.

I bless you in your greening time when dreams begin to shape. May it colour for you the vision of the cowslip in her prime.

I bless you in your changing time when grass gives way to hay. May it give you the freedom of the heart that shares.

I bless you in your victory time of finishing the game. May it fill you with the thirst of beginning to grow again.

I bless you in your meadow time when they ask you for your bread. May it yield in you a hundredfold of every special thing.

THE BLESSING OF THE BOG

You make springs flow in the valleys,
and rivers run between the hills. They
provide water for the wild animals; there
the wild donkeys quench their thirst.

Psalms 104:10-12

Bog Thoughts

The Orange Tip Butterfly was on fire with
freedom. Life on the wing was full of
possibilities and learning. As he spread his
wings to the limits of a butterfly's stretch he
experienced a desire to flit beyond the horizon
but the utter sweetness of the rhododendron
quietened his desire and he remained in his
bog patch. While he delighted in the nibbles
of sheer delight a bog orchid blew some
perfume toward him. The distraction was
designed to lure the butterfly from his local
feeding branch, that he might experience a

new scent. The fragrance of the orchid had an immediate and almost hypnotic effect on the Orange Tip. He was drawn into a beauty beyond himself. He felt himself gliding to and fro, tasting the one, smelling the other, flattering both, until he finally became intoxicated by the sweet distractions of life on the bog. He was fast forgetting the possibility of scaling the horizon and his wings were losing tone from his busy schedule. A resting snipe had been watching the butterfly in an amused kind of way. The snipe wanted to show the butterfly that he alone held the secret of the bog, so he ascended majestically from his resting place, and high in the sky he began a spectacular display of feather vibration until his drumming filled the entire headland. The butterfly was speechless and as he was drawn more and more into the drumming beat he began to fly towards the snipe. Alas! His tiny wings failed him as he tried desperately to imitate the winging of the snipe and he flopped dead weight to the ground. It was the great soft bloom of the rhododendron that saved him. As he regained his breath and went back to sweet nibbles the Orange Tip was enchanted by the call of a corncrake.

— I Bless You —

I bless you on the bog pass. May you find the softest heather in the marshes of your life.
I bless you in the swampy places. May you find a stepping-stone when the earth gives way beneath you.
I bless you at the bog hole. May you find a friend to raise you when you feel you're going down.
I bless you with the bog cotton. May you sit beside the turf-cutter and sense the plan of time.
I bless you with the curlew cry. May you hear your inner voice as you cross the silent moor.
I bless you with the turtledoves. May your loss become discovery as you circle on the wind.
I bless you with the elder berries. May you taste the bread and wine as you gather with the neighbours for the breakfast on the bog.
I bless you with the timeless seam that gives a pattern to your bog. May you breathe in the air of life and may God bless all the turf.

WORDS OF BLESSING

For Joseph

God almighty blesses Joseph
with blessings from heaven above,
with blessings from the deep below,
with blessings of the breast and the womb.
The blessings of your father, greater than the
blessings of the ancient mountains, than the
bounty of the everlasting hills.
May they all rest on the head of Joseph,
on the brow of the one who is a prince among
brothers.

Genesis 49:25

For Abraham

I will make a covenant between myself and
you, and I will multiply your race.
You will be the father of a multitude of
nations.
No longer will you be called Abram, but
Abraham because I will make you the father of

a multitude of nations.
I will make you more and more famous;
I will multiply your descendants.
Nations shall spring from you; kings shall be
among your descendants.
And I will establish a covenant,
an everlasting covenant between myself and
you and your descendants after you, for
generations to come.
I will give you and your descendants after you
the land you are living in, all the land of
Canaan, as an everlasting possession and I will
be the God of your race.

Genesis 17:1-8

CHAPTER TWO

*The Blessing of the Songbird,
of the Vine, of the Lamb*

The Blessing of the Songbird

Sing to the Lord, all the world!
Worship God with joy;
Come before him with happy songs

Psalm 100

Bird Thoughts

I am the Songbird. I was born to sing in the hedges and in the laneways. In order to keep the song alive I praise God in the morning of the day and the people wake with me for the dawn chorus. My song is of oceans and mountain peaks, of journeys and of destinies. I carry nothing on my back and I need neither road nor compass because God who clothes the grasses cares even more for me, the Songbird. I am the Songbird. I know all the shapes of the sea and her tides. I know the secrets of the currents and the hospitality of the winds. From the sky I see the whole picture and the distance gives me a fresh perspective. I am richly blessed for my wings free me from the pull downward and they take me safely through the clouds. The ocean test brings out the best in me; I know how small the ocean is and over and over my spirit endures the long goodbyes.

I am the Songbird. I am a flock creature and I have learned in my life about the strength of numbers. I fly with other songbirds and I mingle with doves and eagles. We have mastered the art of sharing the skies and we have seen that the birds who survive make the journey together. When the soil is in her wintertime we share the seeds with the farmyard folk. The families invite us to the bird table with nuts and fat and crumbs of richest food. I am the Songbird. I give God thanks in every season. I sing on the rooftop; I dance on the wind and I harmonise the chorus. My song is my identity and I practice until the notes are sweet with tenderness and feeling. The right melody attracts the right mate and when the evening falls the angels gather to sing their lullaby, for the Songbird.

— I Bless You —

I bless you with my blue feathers. May you
find shelter from violent forces.

I bless you with my white breast. May you find
comfort when you are tired.

I bless you with my yellow bill. May you find
food to nourish your spirit.

I bless you with my highest note. May you find
your highest star.

I bless you with my dawn song. May you find
sunlight in your life.

I bless you with my torn feet. May you find a
song for your journey.

I bless you with my wing speed. May you find
the destiny of your dream.

I bless you with my ocean compass. May you
find the direction of your heart.

I bless you with my farseeing eye. May you
find vision in your darkness.

I bless you with my bird courage. May you
find strength in your tidal wave.

I bless you with my companion birds. May you
find someone to love you.

I bless you with my Mother God. May you
find in God a mother's care.

I bless you with my Father God. May you find
in God a father's protection.

I bless you with my brother Jesus. May you
find in him a faithful friend.

THE BLESSING OF THE VINE

*The plant sprouted and became a low,
wide-spreading grapevine. The branches
grew upward toward the eagle, and the
roots grew deep. The vine was covered
with branches and leaves.*

Ezekiel 17:5-6

Vine Thoughts

The young vine did not like the idea of having
to spread out and creep along slowly until the
wire netting and all the thin wooden stakes were
completely covered with foliage. It preferred the
way that apples and potatoes grew; it seemed
more practical and efficient to the creeping vine.
The vine often felt that life was dull and that
growing up was taking too long. The older
grape vines kept reminding the young one that
in life, the creeping becomes the climbing and
that good creepers become good climbers. The
young vine was not just creeping; it was

discovering its own unique flavour and the quality of wine it would one day bring to the feast. The young vine kept returning to this advice when the creeping became really boring. It is a slow, painstaking process, taking three years for the grapes to be brought to birth. The senior vines asked the young one to focus on the wonderful things that happen to it during the creeping years. It's green luxuriant foliage, for example, provides excellent shade and gives new aspect to the garden. The young vine's unique ability to wrap itself around any available support makes even the broken-down fence look attractive. The young vine learns the great lessons of life in its creeping times, lessons about pruning and reaching out for support. When it yields its plans to the wisdom of the gardener who guides the twining and the holding fast, the young vine comes to enlightenment. It learns the secret of becoming the best that a vine can be The wisdom of the elders assured the young vines that they were not just creeping along; they were filling the garden.

— I Bless You —

I bless you with the Root of the vine. May you never be afraid to reach out into the deep.

I bless you with the Stem of the vine. May it attach you to the source of life.

I bless you with the Leaves of the vine. May you find shelter in the support of good friends and may you be a shelter for those who have lost direction.

I bless you with the Sap of the vine. May you find faith, friendship and food to sustain the life in you.

I bless you with the Taste of the vine. May you give beauty and colour and all good things.

I bless you with the Life of the vine. May your smiles, your opinions and your presence be life-giving.

I bless you with the Clinging of the vine. May your faith hold on for you when the fence gives way.

I bless you with the Pace of the vine. May your footsteps give you time to weave your love into the soil of the earth.

I bless you with the Fruit of the vine. May the love of God flow in you and through you and from you.

May the love of God fill your fields with plenty and may God's love be the vineyard of your harvest.

THE BLESSING OF THE LAMB

To him who sits on the throne and to the
Lamb,
Be praise and honour, glory and might,
for ever and ever.

Revelation 5:13

Lamb Thoughts

The sheep was unable to feed her lamb so the
shepherd gave him the baby's bottle. The lamb
was cautious at first, mixing closely with human
tenderness, but he decided that if he were to
survive he would have to partake of their food
and drink from their bottles. In time the lamb
learned to play with the children and to dance
with them in the meadows. The other lambs
were worried at the gradual humanisation of
their fellow lamb and they especially disliked
the way in which he began to talk to the
wolfhound and to stand thoughtfully like a
shepherd. The little lamb learned many

interesting things from life in the pasture and from life in the farmer's kitchen. He learned to bleat like the needy and he learned that every fence has a potential opening. As the months passed he began to put on a lot of weight. This was a difficult time for a growing lamb as the butcher had a particular fondness for fat lambs.

He wanted to enjoy the family gatherings and be part of the fun and laughter but he could tell with every passing day that they liked him better when he was a harmless baby. It was something about his inner strength, his fearlessness, his influence with the other lambs, that bothered them. He still remembers that day when he stood in the rain, crying with hunger, but no one gave him a bottle. The thought crossed his mind to leave the farmyard for ever and to return to the wild goats on the mountainside but he decided to make one last effort to restore the bond of friendship with the humans. He promised to become a shepherd himself and to mind the farmer's sheep, if he could just remain part of the family.

— I Bless You —

Behold the Lamb of God! May he bless you in your beginning times and give you a brave heart.

Behold the Lamb of God! May he bless you in your fragile times and give you a helping hand.

Behold the Lamb of God! May he bless you in your trusting times and give you a faithful friend.

Behold the Lamb of God! May he bless you in your fearful times and give you a quiet pasture.

Behold the Lamb of God! May he bless you in your lost times and give you a shepherd's care.

Behold the Lamb of God! May he bless you in your hungry times and give you a touch of love.

Behold the Lamb of God! May he bless you in your homeless times and give you a place to belong.

Behold the Lamb of God! May he bless you in your dancing times and give you a prophet's song.

Behold the Lamb of God! May he bless you in your loving times and give you a joy without ending.

Words of Blessing

For the Sabbath

In six days God made the heavens and the
earth, the seas and all that is in them.
But on the seventh day he rested.
That is why God has blessed the seventh day
and made it holy.
The Sabbath is a sign between myself and you
from generation to generation to show that it
is I, Yahweh, who have made you my own
people.
You must keep the Sabbath, then; it is to be
held sacred by you.

Exodus 20:11; 31:13-14

For the People

May God bless you and keep you.
May God let his face shine on you.
May God be gracious to you.
May God look kindly on you.

May God give you peace.
With these words you shall put my name on
the people and I will bless them.

Numbers 6:22-27

For the Faithful Ones

You will be blessed in your city and in your
fields.
You will be blessed in your children and in
your livestock.
You will be blessed in your cooking and in
your eating.
You will be blessed in your beginning and in
your finishing.
You will be blessed in your granaries and in
your activities.
Yahweh shall open the heavens to you to give
rain in its season and he shall bless all that you
plan to do.

Deuteronomy 28:3-11

CHAPTER THREE

The Blessing of the Wood,
of the River, of Marriage

THE BLESSING OF THE WOOD

Behold the wood of the cross on which hung the Saviour of the world! Come let us worship.

Good Friday Liturgy

Wood Thoughts

As part of the great forest I cannot help thinking that life endures. I have heard the people talking about the shortness of time and about the passing of things from sight, but my story is of enduring, and of going on and of linking generations. This perspective, I know, has something to do with deep roots. The old dining-room table could explain it better than me. She has hosted tea parties and dinner parties, communion parties and confirmation parties, baptism parties and ordination parties. Her wood was the gift of the old oak tree that grew for two hundred years until it yielded to the craftsman to become a meeting place. The other trees and shrubs missed her safe shelter and her gracious presence in the forest. She handled the endless change of season into season with the wisdom of age and the calmness of noble hearts. It was the great oak that one day embraced the call of autumn to let go and become a new creation. Having withstood the storms of life that stripped the forest and dismantled the law and order, the oak tree was ready to cross over. She had given her life to others. The wind had played music in her branches. The sun had painted patterns on her greenery and the children had built their hiding places in her warm embrace. The great oak had shown very special care for God's little creatures who found a safe home with her. The carpenter was careful with the oak tree and as the great champion fell to the ground he dreamed of beautiful things like family tables and church altars and sacred carvings. He would make sure that the magnificence endured because he knew that the plan of God was written in the wood of a tree.

— I Bless You —

When the shadows hide the light, may the
wood bless you with patience.
When the work of the day tires you, may the
wood bless you with renewal.
When the rains wash away your dreams, may
the wood bless you with strength.
When the wind blows against your best
efforts, may the wood bless you with standing
still.
When the fire burns your plan to ashes, may
the wood bless you with glowing embers.
When the carpenter cuts you to measure, may
the wood bless you with handing over.
When the seasons challenge you to keep
changing may the wood bless you with new
shoots.
When your song is silenced, may the wood
bless you with a softer melody.
When the cross touches you, may the wood
bless you with the arms of Christ.
When the tomb closes, may the wood bless
you with her resurrection story.

The Blessing of the River

*As the scripture says, 'Whoever believes
in me, rivers of living water will pour
out from his heart'.*

John 7:38

River Thoughts

The river was happy in the headwaters with the other small streams. They mingled gently in a dozing way, under the noonday sun and thoughts of seas and oceans were faraway dreams. The river, however, was aware of his growing fullness and one day he brimmed over and began to trickle down the fairy hill. The first trickle soon became a stream and with the sloping land the stream became a river. This is what he was meant to be, a river! The other sleeping rivers were critical of their adventurous colleague. He was going too far, spreading out over the land, forming a channel for himself and daring to aim for the ocean. This was, they believed, quite arrogant of a little river.

41

The river, once free from his sleeping companions, made steady progress. He began to cross boundaries and to melt rocks. The people built bridges to new places and flowers began to grow in the wasteland. The river began to discover other forms of life. Otters and dragonflies, bulrushes and reeds came to befriend him. They said that the river had brought them new questions. There was a growing excitement in the countryside as the river flowed southwards toward the open gorge, and when he cascaded in torrents to the depths below the hope of electrical power came to the rural people. The river was alive with joy. He was bringing forth abundance and making connections and repairing the landscape. He had become an energy for life, and flora and fauna, insects and fish were blessing the God of the river.

The other rivers were getting uncomfortable now as news flowed back to them that their daring comrade was already close to the ocean. Some of the rivers began to question their own lives of stagnant waiting so they decided to call a conference of rivers in order to explore the dangers of a river's journey to the ocean. As the rivers worked diligently on a process for their way forward the morning newspaper carried a picture of a little river entering the ocean.

− I Bless You −

When the river of life calls you to life, may God bless you with joy.
When the river of life calls you to begin, may God bless you with courage.
When the river of life calls you to flow, may God bless you with direction.
When the river of life calls you to turn, may God bless you with faith.
When the river of life calls you to tumble down, may God bless you with delight.
When the river of life calls you to let go, may God bless you with generosity.
When the river of life calls you to spread out, may God bless you with wisdom.
When the river of life calls you to share yourself, may God bless you with insight.
When the river of life calls you to change course, may God bless you with vision.
When the river of life calls you to settle down, may God bless you with gratitude.
When the river of life calls you to yield to the ocean, may God bless you with fulfilment.

The Blessing of Marriage

*Love never gives up and its faith, hope
and patience never fail.*

1 Corinthians 13

Marriage Thoughts

God first loved us. Love is God's way. It is the decision to look beyond the limitations of single insights and to be enriched by another perspective, to be deepened by another dimension. Love is the response of a generous attitude that understands the essential pulse of life as a giving and receiving. Love desires the music of harmony where songs are blended and where lyrics are shared stories. It is the energy of the mutual action and it is the desire of the incomplete experience. Love longs to be together where stars twinkle alone in the vast galaxy and love needs to be nourished where difference is celebrated and where joy is doubled.

Love is always now. It travels safely in the heart as a trusted companion. It is there to open locked doors, to close widening gaps, to scale dividing walls, to moisten the frozen earth. Love is never an easy option but it is always a best option. It knows the right time and the waiting time and the holding time and the letting-go time. Love never keeps for itself; it is the river of life, awakening the landscape, easing the thirst, releasing the colours.

Love is to covenant called because the nature of love is to connect with trust and to be faithful with promise. Since time began love has provided themes for writers and artists, for buyers and for sellers but it is still known only to those who hold the rose on the thorn and who give without counting the cost.

When I said 'I do' with a silver ring I thought for an instant of the great circles of sun and moon, of beginnings and of endings. I thought of our love and how it links us to the eternal communion.

– I Bless You –

May God bless your giving with abundance.
May God bless your receiving with deep
appreciation.
May God bless your trusting with confidence.
May God bless your hoping with many
blessings.
May God bless your promise with faithfulness.
May God bless your house with touches of
home.
May God bless your relating with gentleness.
May God bless your decisions with mutuality.
May God bless your listening with openness.
May God bless your speaking with reverence.
May God bless your companionship with
warm friendship.
May God bless your sorrows with inner
strength.
May God bless your laughter with shared
delight.
May God bless your praying with stillness.
May God bless your loving with communion
of your spirits. Amen.

Words of Blessing

For Remembering

I called you from your mother's womb. I
pronounced your name before you were born
and hid you in the shadow of my hand.
I will make you the light of the nations that
my salvation will reach the ends of the earth.
You will be my covenant with the people and
they will find pasture on barren hills.
They will neither hunger nor thirst, nor will
the scorching wind nor the sun beat upon
them.
For I who am merciful will lead them to
springs of living water.
Can a woman forget the baby at her breast and
have no compassion on the child of her
womb?
Yet though she forget, I will never forget you.

Isaiah 49

For Faithfulness

I will come to you and fulfil my promise of
restoring you.
I know my plans for you, plans to save you and
not to harm you, plans to give you a future
and to give you hope.
When you call me, I will listen.
When you search for me with your heart you
will find me.
I will let myself be found by you and I will
gather you from among all the nations and
bring you home.

Jeremiah 29:10-14

CHAPTER FOUR

*The Blessing of Friends,
of Sabbath Light, of Baptism*

The Blessing of Friends

I thank God for you every time I think
of you.
And every time I pray for you I pray
with joy.

Philippians 2:3

Friend Thoughts

I will be with you for ever and for always.
Walking beside you, shoulder to shoulder, I
keep pace with your footsteps. When you
disappear from view I trust you to the angel of
light and I allow you to find other paths and to
follow your lone star. The space between us is
our togetherness; and the space above us is our
closeness. We do not seek to be together in time;
we desire to be together in seeking and in
searching until the days are timeless. Your
dreams are sacred to me and with my heart I
give you wings to fly upward and outward, away
from me that you may return to replenish
friendship's cup for another journey. It does not
matter to me how far you fly, for time and

distance reveal the freedom of our friendship.

I want to be a presence in your life, one that draws you out to become your finest expression. I desire to call you forth, to awaken the richness of your ability, to stretch the distance of your vision. I am the space between your joy and your sorrow, a lifeline connection in your story. I do not tell your story, nor do I shape it; but at the turn of each chapter I honour your effort and I suggest new titles. When you fall down I speak to you of your strength and when you climb the heights I speak to you of your blessings. When the laughter in your heart bursts out I sing the harmony of your song and when your pathway closes in, I hold your hand.

We will be connected for ever and for always because we have understood about letting go, about returning the beast to the wilderness, about allowing the bird her nest in the treetop. I give you the promise dear friend, and you give me the possibility.

— I Bless You —

I bless you dear friend with the staff of
Patrick. May he give you a mountain view.
I bless you dear friend with the mantle of
Brigid. May she widen your landscape.
I bless you dear friend with the vision of
Brendan. May he keep your dream alive.
I bless you dear friend with the strength of
Abraham. May he lead you outward.
I bless you dear friend with the wisdom of
Solomon. May he guide your decisions.
I bless you dear friend with the patience of
Job. May he help you in your struggle.
I bless you dear friend with the courage of
Peter. May he show you how to lead.
I bless you dear friend with the generosity of
Martha. May she help you in your work.
I bless you dear friend with the love of
Thérèse. May she open your heart to others.
I bless you dear friend with the faith of
Monica. May she teach you to keep trying.
I bless you dear friend with the work of
Joseph. May he shape your inner journey.
I bless you dear friend with the arms of Mary.
May she speak to you of joy.
I bless you dear friend with the heart of Jesus.
May he hold you safely, always.

THE BLESSING OF SABBATH LIGHT

Observe the Sabbath and keep it holy.
You have six days in which to do your
work but the seventh day is a day of rest
dedicated to me.

Exodus 20

Sabbath Thoughts

It is time to rest. The setting sun marks the Sabbath hour. The evening silence is filled with silent adoration and the family gathers to light the Sabbath candle. The father announces that the sacred rhythm of the week has ended and the mother holds the holy light. The ancient psalms of Jewish praise connect us again with our faith line, ancient as Abraham, holy as Mary. We are retelling the story tonight as we stand faithfully in the depth of the Sabbath light. The light is full of stillness. God is here and we know it.

Light of Christ, light of heaven and earth, fill our Sabbath time with prayer. May all our fears be ended as we pause in this holy rest with you. Draw our souls into the holiness of this hour and open in our longing a desire for rest in God.

As the great light fills the room, the church, the countryside, every space, the people gather. They are born of an ancient heritage, old as the faith of prophets, ageless as the cosmic dust. The Sabbath Light reminds them that they are God's people; it is the sign for all time that they belong to God. This is more than their day of rest; it is their day of remembering and of thanksgiving. The Sabbath experience is a vital moment in keeping life human. It calls us back into God's time and space, into the one who authors life from its origin to its endpoint. Without our Sabbath time the routine of hours and days chase each other round and round in circles of busyness, without ever going forward. So we light the Sabbath Light to enter more deeply into the holy place. We close down our other options and bless the God of our resting time.

— I Bless You —

God of our Sabbath Light, bless us at this
holy hour.
Bless the shepherds of the Church with
Sabbath light.
Bless the lonely people with Sabbath light.
Bless the families who gather with Sabbath
light.
Bless our neighbourhood with Sabbath light.

God of our Sabbath Light, bless us at this
holy hour.
Bless the busyness of our time with Sabbath
light.
Bless the stillness of this evening with Sabbath
light.
Bless the anxiety of our fears with Sabbath
light.
Bless the nations of the earth with Sabbath
light.

God of our Sabbath Light, bless us at this
holy hour.
Bless our Jewish brothers and sisters with
Sabbath light.
Bless our struggle for reconciliation with
Sabbath light.
Bless seekers and searchers with Sabbath light.
Bless all creation with Sabbath light.

The Blessing of Baptism

After Jesus had been baptised by John the heavens opened and the Holy Spirit descended on him in bodily shape, like a dove, and a voice came from heaven: You are my beloved Son, on you my favour rests.

Matthew 3

Baptism Thoughts

This is the beginning. The Christian era is inaugurated in the River Jordan. Jesus goes down into the pool of human pain and confusion, to immerse himself in the muddied water. Here in the river of human encounter Jesus meets his people. As he goes down into the water we know that he has accepted us and that he has identified himself with our brokenness. This moment of acceptance is our day of hope and every baptism ever after will flow from the Jordan river.

The people are coming to the river. Every pathway is jammed. They want to go down with him, to take on his life as he has taken on their life. They want to stand beside him as he is named a 'beloved son' and to hear their own names spoken from the heavens. They are coming to the river with a great thirst for identity and for belonging. As the water covers them there is a stirring in their awareness and the cleansing reaches their very hearts.

Then he said, 'I baptise you'. I give you a deeper life. I welcome you to my own family. I form a bond with you for ever. I sign your body with the sign of my own loving and together we will die and together we will rise. 'I baptise you.' With holy oil I number you among the priests, prophets, kings and queens of the ancient story. In this river I crown you in the dignity of the angels, for this is a new life and you are a new creation.

The Spirit of God hovered over the water and the Breath brought back freshness and joy to the people. As they left the Jordan that day they walked back home, together.

— I Bless You —

I bless your search with the Light of Christ.
May it burn eternally in your life.

I bless your journey with the Sign of Christ.
May it protect you at every moment.

I bless your struggle with the Water of Christ.
May it wash away your sins.

I bless your footstep with the Oil of Christ.
May it strengthen your purpose.

I bless your days with the Holiness of Christ.
May it sanctify your decisions.

I bless your speaking with the Mind of Christ.
May it soften your responses.

I bless your hearing with the Heart of Christ.
May it open your understanding.

I bless your loving with the Blood of Christ.
May it deepen your promise.

I bless your working with the Hand of Christ.
May it ease your burden.

I bless your playing with the Laughter of Christ.
May it rest your spirit.

I bless your thinking with the Gentleness of
Christ. May it unlock your insight.

I bless your fearing with the Calmness of
Christ. May it heal your anxiety.

I bless your hoping with the Victory of Christ.
May it lead you to your destiny.

WORDS OF BLESSING

For Friendship

*Do not ask me to leave you, for I will go
where you go, and stay where you stay.
Your people will be my people, and your
god will be my God. Wherever you die I
shall die and be buried.*

Ruth 1:16-18

For Wisdom

Blessed be wisdom who singles out the good
people and keeps them steadfast.
Blessed be wisdom who stands with the
upright person against the greed of oppressors.
Blessed be wisdom who gives to holy people
the wages of their labour.
Blessed be wisdom who gives us shade during
the day and the light of the stars by night.
Blessed be wisdom who led her people across
the Red Sea and through the wilderness.
Blessed be wisdom who gave her people water

from a rocky cliff to relieve their parched spirits.
Blessed be wisdom who gave her people water
in abundance.

Wisdom 11

For Friends

I bless you with the gentle word that makes
many friends.
I bless you with the agreeable tongue that calls
forth gracious replies.
I bless you with a seeing eye that knows a
faithful friend.
I bless you with a friend at table who is
steadfast in adversity.
I bless you with a secure refuge in the company
of your friend.
I bless you with a rich treasure that is a trusted
friend.
I bless you with the priceless gift, a friend
without price.
I bless you with a sense of God, for as you are
so will your friends be.

Sirach 6:5-17

CHAPTER FIVE

The Blessing of Loss,
of a Teardrop, of Mary

The Blessing of Loss

I am the resurrection and the life.
If anyone believes in me, even though he
dies, he will live, and whoever lives and
believes in me will never die.

John 11

Loss Thoughts

Today I sit at the tomb of earth and the great stone separates you from me. You are gone now without an address, without a geographical space. The hush, the terror, the night, the chill are upon me. Every roadway is covered in and the sky is grey with darkness. This is the night hour that they spoke about and life is grinding to a halt. There is a power failure in my heart and the night comes early and lingers on. In the depths of my spirit the temperature has fallen rapidly. The kitchen table is strangely bare except for the stained coffee mug. Sometimes I drop a spoon just to hear the noise. I am too cold to go to bed and I fear the absence so I walk back, again, to the large slab of granite that marks the spot and it seems to support the weight of my grief.

The stone is standing firm against my deepest protests. It is somehow holding on for me and in its lifeless mass it speaks to me of endurance. I put the full weight of my body against the polished slab, cold on cold, and then the strangest thing happens: the grass at my feet begins to talk to me! It tells me of its journey from under the great rock, how it waited and pushed and went on breathing against the greatest weight. One day the grass saw a tiny light coming from the sun; it seemed to pass freely through the marble stone and at that moment the grass knew that she had not been dead at all, just waiting for a new beginning. As I lifted my body from the tombstone on that February morning I raised my eyes to the sky and the sun was there and I began to feel warm again.

– I Bless You –

The universe reveals the magnificence of God.
May the splendour of creation bless you with
stillness.
The earth holds the promise of new life. May
the promise bless you with hope.
The steadfast rock reminds you of your secret
strength. May the rock bless you with strong
thoughts.
The longest shadow closes down in the rising
sun. May the shadow lead you into the
morning.
The soft teardrop releases the pain. May the
teardrop restore your tender feeling.
The warm sunlight stirs the frozen heart. May
the sunlight bless you with warm embraces.
The voice of an angel keeps pace with your
heavy step. May your angel bless you with
wings to fly again.
The love of Mary's heart feels your pain. May
Mary bless you with an enduring faith.
The arms of Jesus' sorrow holds you. May
Jesus bless you through the darkness.

The Blessing of a Teardrop

Blessed are those who mourn;
They shall be comforted.

Matthew 5

Teardrop Thoughts

I was just a tiny drop when I fell the long journey from your eyelid right down to your cheekbone and I left that tiny furrow, moist and creased. The journey was slow and although I am only a teardrop I carried the weight of your heart. You wiped me away in case others might follow and then you might cry and never stop. It was easier for you to stand and shiver in the cold graveyard air, frozen and dry-eyed as the wind blew me away, far away. But I am your teardrop and I am part of you. I fill up your eyes and I tell what words cannot imagine. I fill up your eyes and your memories flow gently downstream. I am not to be feared because I record your story with all its feelings and with all its seasons. I am the face of your deepest

response. I am the secret of your sacred space. In joy and in sorrow, in longing and in peace I bring your moments to their brimming over.
I am your teardrop.

Although I am very small I bring growth and nourishment to the garden of your soul. Where I fall the soil is vulnerable and porous and the seeds of your planting seek a deeper rooting. I do not want to flood your fields; I desire only to bring you to the richest harvest where teardrops merge with the ocean in the great communion of heaven and earth.

You feel unplugged now, stuck to the ground with stripped wires but I am your teardrop and I will flow for you and I will cry for you and I will speak for you and one day soon you will let me fall unhindered and I will wet your lips.

— I Bless You —

You stood on the earth and walked with the
confidence of an oak tree.
May God bless you until we meet again.
We sheltered in your strength for you were free
from the common fears.
May God bless you until we meet again.
Your pace was steady and full of purpose as
you kept your focus clear.
May God bless you until we meet again.
You filled the empty space and now it longs
for your presence.
May God bless you until we meet again.
You dreamed with the eyes of a big heart and
you spoke in different colours.
May God bless you until we meet again.
You opened the story to a new understanding
and you believed in new chapters.
May God bless you until we meet again.
You had a capacity for difference, for holding
the balance.
May God bless you until we meet again.
Your spirit was intimate and free, resilient and
expansive.
May God bless you until we meet again.
Your faith was strong and humble, full with
questions.
May God bless you until we meet again.

The Blessing of Mary

I am the handmaiden of God;
let it be done to me as God says.

Luke 1:38

Mary Thoughts

In God's time I was chosen. I was still very young and very vulnerable and I wondered what God saw in me? I was free to decline this sacred thrust but I was aware of our ancient history and I knew about Abraham and Moses and Sara and Miriam and how they had believed the unbelievable and followed their God to journey's end. My decision would also affect every waking hour for the rest of my life. I did not know the why nor the how but I accepted the now moment.

It was difficult for me to grasp the power of God at work in such an ordinary place as Nazareth. We were a mountain people in step with the primal elements. The rhythm of our lives was predictable and constant and a combination of healthy climate and good food gave us a strong, robust look.

When I was fifteen years my parents made plans for my betrothal to Joseph, the carpenter. Joseph seemed like a gentle man to me and he was greatly respected in the village. I felt privileged to have my life linked with his and I was full of joy at the thought of my own home and children and farm animals. But then something happened!

It happens in every life. There is a life-altering moment when the songs of childhood resound with a new and mysterious call and the village well is deeper than we ever imagined and the heart swells with love's response. It happened to me and I too was brought face to face with the question of the divine. In that moment of unknowing, God moved into my awareness and linked his life to mine.

I gave my life to the mystery and in the giving I received in my body the Light that filled the world.

— I Bless You —

I bless your annunciation time. May your
response be generous with love.
I bless your visitation time. May your concern
be selfless with hospitality.
I bless your invitation time. May your gift-
giving be great with kindness.
I bless your journey time. May your fatigue be
lessened with expectation.
I bless your difficult time. May your loved
ones understand with you.
I bless your family time. May your
togetherness be a sacred space.
I bless your homeless time. May your own
heart shelter you.
I bless your Bethlehem time. May your joy be
complete with giving birth.
I bless your Egypt time. May your anxiety be
eased with letting go.
I bless your Cana time. May your faith endure
when the wine runs out.
I bless your goodbye time. May your children
carry the light you gave them.
I bless your Calvary time. May your cross
reveal your inner strength.
I bless your resurrection time. May you live
forever with God.

Words of Blessing

For Nature

The sun shines on everything and reveals the blessings of God.
God blesses the depth of the abyss and the human heart with the secrets of God.
God blesses the signs in the heavens with the knowledge of God.
God blesses the past and the future with the mystery of God.
God blesses the marvellous works of creation with the wisdom of God.
God blesses the smallest spark of light with the beauty of God.
God blesses all living things with the unity of God.
God bless the universe with the excellence of God.
Who could ever weary of admiring God's glory?

Sirach 42:16-25

For Trust

Rejoice in the Lord, you who are just,
praise is fitting for loyal hearts.
Give thanks to God on the harp and lyre
making melody and chanting praises.
God's word is upright and worthy of our trust.
God loves justice and fills the earth with
kindness.
The heavens were created by the word of God
who stores the waters of the deep in cellars.
The plan of God stands forever
and his heart's design through all generations.
God gazes on those who fear him.
On those who trust in God's loving kindness,
there will be no death and they will be safe from
famine.
We wait in hope for the Lord for he is our help
and our shield.
Our hearts rejoice for all our trust is in God's
holy name.

Psalm 33

For God with us

God is our strength and our protection, always
with us. Even if the earth be shaken and
mountains plunge into the seas and waters foam
and roar, and mountains quake and totter, still,
we will not fear. God is with us.

Psalms 46

CHAPTER SIX

The Blessing of Hearing, of Work

The Blessing of Hearing

*So, then, anyone who hears these words of
mine and acts accordingly is like a wise
person, who built his house on rock.*

Matthew 7

Hearing Thoughts

The bowl is empty. The well is dry. The people
bite the dust. There is silence where the masses
huddle for shelter. Where have all the raindrops
gone? Where have all the promises gone? I hear
the pleading and the crying of the withered
grass. I hear the wrinkled skin on dried bones.
It is a sound like breaking pieces. I hear it and
my spirit trembles.

The bowl is empty. The well is dry. They
have walked for years, believing in another
chance, hoping for another day. You avoid the
baby's eyes. Your breasts are dry and you feel
responsible as innocent people feel the guilt.
The baby's life will pass as swiftly as the evening
shadows, his cheeks cold with anger. I hear the

ebbing away of little whimpers and my ears are full of discord and distress.

The bowl is empty. The well is dry. We have treated them with cruelty and our abject greed has become their intolerable poverty. You walk slowly now, carrying the whole family on your back. You keep moving forward for there is food in the distance. Your feet shuffle and you eyes stare to stay open but you keep moving forward into the distance. I hear the wail of desert sand as it grinds out noises on your empty plate. The flies and the vultures keep pace with the drooping pace. I hear their still flight, waiting to descend.

The bowl is empty. The well is dry. I hear the sin of my time devouring the land, stripping the forest bare. It grasps and holds; it chokes and kills. I hear it now. My ears are full of horror.

— I Bless You —

You named my oppressor and I went free: I
bless your name.
You sent me bread and wine: I bless your name.
You gave me clean water and opened a well in
my heart: I bless your name.
You taught my children to read and to laugh: I
bless your name.
You spoke to me of God and I learned to
hope: I bless your name.
You gave me a chance in life and I planted
seeds: I bless your name.
You believed in me and in my ability to begin
again: I bless your name.
You welcomed me and called my name: I bless
your name.
You sat at the table with me and passed me the
water: I bless your name.
You took away my guilt and I tasted life: I
bless your name.
You remembered me in prison and you heard
my story: I bless your name.
You sat at my bedside and listened with
compassion: I bless your name.
You stayed through the night and watched
with me: I bless your name.
You taught me how to pray and now I thirst: I
bless your name.

THE BLESSING OF WORK

*The Jews persecuted Jesus because he
performed healings like that on the
Sabbath. Jesus replied, 'My Father goes on
working and so do I'.*

John 5:17

Work Thoughts

God said 'Let there be Light', and work began.
It was a shaping and a sculpturing, a colouring
and a breathing in the silence of the void. The
work began to generate abundance and to
awaken a desire for communion. The empty
space groaned for the first time and the story of
'God with us' began to unfold. There was
communion in the forest and the waters
embraced the land in a primal instinct to share
their resources. The work ethic developed and
living things began to experience their
uniqueness and their connections as they
reached out and dug deep. Work became the call
of life, to give and to receive, to nourish and to

77

be nourished. It held the sacred space together for the emerging web of relationships. The balanced rhythm of resting and of striving became the rhythm of nature and God brought forth the woman and the man to be stewards of the dream and to cultivate the garden of life. This was the partnership of God with the people and the work of human hearts forged this intimate bonding and brought out the best in us.

The birds gathered twigs for their nesting time and the sheep protected the lambs in their growing time. The cat hunted through the night and the bee filled the honeycomb. Every mind and every heart expanded and the possibilities were written in every space. The digger and the potter, the dreamer and the baker were all drawn into the partnership. The mother worked the dough and houses became homes. The father worked the fields and every meal became a communion. The relationship intensified and the dignity and the destiny of the work was captured in the paintings, in the melodies, in the sowing and in the harvest.

— I Bless You —

I bless the wood of the carpenter. May the
chair that you fashion become a welcome seat.
I bless the spade of the gardener. May the seed
that you sow become a bouquet of flowers.
I bless the fingers of the musician. May the
songs that you play become a living harmony.
I bless the skill of the doctor. May the healing
that you bring become an ode to life.
I bless the awareness of the fire fighter. May
the risks that you take become a timeless
memory.
I bless the knowledge of the teacher. May the
lessons that you learn become a stepping stone
for others.
I bless the heart of the mother and father.
May the love that you generate become the
hope of the nations.

WORDS OF BLESSING

For Disciples

Blessed are those who refer all experience to
God; the kingdom of heaven is theirs.
Blessed are those who experience
incompleteness; they shall be comforted.
Blessed are those who reject violence in word
and deed; they shall possess the land.
Blessed are those who liberate oppressive
systems; they shall be satisfied.
Blessed are those who hear the other side of
the story; they shall find mercy.
Bless are those who carry no malice; they shall
see God.
Blessed are those who respect all people and
things; they shall be called children of God.
Blessed are those who put their lives on the
line for justice; theirs is the kingdom of
heaven.

Matthew 5:3-10

For the Meal

We followed you on foot to a lonely place
because we were hungry and you saw us as we
gathered on the shore. We were a huddled
mass, spent in the heat of the day and wanting
a place in your line of vision.
I remember your compassion that late
afternoon and how you reached out to the sick
people with your eyes and with your strength.
We just kept coming across the valley, in our
thousands, and you kept drawing us into the
embrace. As the sun began to yield to the
evening I noticed an anxiety in your disciples.
They knew that hungry people can become
frustrated and even violent and they wanted us
out of the place. I often recall your words to
them, 'You give them something to eat'. The
rest of the story is vague to me now but you
did manage to fill us that day, each one of us,
on the bread and fish. When it was over we
walked back home, through the night, fearless
and strong, happy and at peace. Even the
disciples were glad that we had stayed. It was a
blessed day. Praise be the God of the meal.

Matthew 14:13-21

CHAPTER SEVEN

*The Blessings of Winter,
of Eucharist*

THE BLESSING OF WINTER

You fixed the earth's borders.
You created summer and winter.

Psalms 74

Winter Thoughts

I cause the land to freeze over and I call the people to stand still. All creation has known her springtime of creative energy and her summertime of blossoming and becoming. Then, as her autumn time of achievement and fruitfulness is harvested, I creep into the stillness, to guard the waiting time. In my deep valley the barren field reveals the timeless mystery and the letting go of the flower, frees the secret of the seed. Sometimes there is fear at my approach and in the failing light all living things face the shadows. But I am not the killer of the dream nor the dark season of depression. I am the season of renewal, the Sabbath of the soul. As your hemisphere inclines away from the sun, you will also find your turning point in the darkest night. In every passing year I hold for all created things the experience of God's abiding presence in the seasons of their lives. I am the visible reminder of light in the darkness and of life from the grave. The scarce times are abundant times as human hearts bring their food to the bird's table. The scarce times are enduring times as the human spirit reaches beyond the limits of drought and hunger. The scarce times are always changing times where something dies and something lives and the tomb of fallen leaves becomes a womb of new beginnings. When I call you into my winter space you will feel your finger tips turn to numbness and you skin will dry in the frozen air but I am your holding time where the new and the old, the endings and the beginnings merge to paint a deeper colour on your canvas. Do not be afraid of my approach; in the longest night there is a dawn awakening.

– I Bless You –

God of our winter sleep, bless your people
with the dawn from on high.
God of our winter passage, bless your people
with direction in difficult times.
God of our winter silence, bless your people
with still moments of prayer.
God of our winter waiting, bless your people
with hope when they cannot see.
God of our winter bareness, bless your people
with seasons of plenty.
God of our winter numbness, bless your
people with kind feeling.
God of our winter solstice, bless your people
with a turning point.
God of our winter tomb, bless your people
with inner light.
God of our winter knowledge, bless your
people with deeper wisdom.
God of our winter sorrow, bless your people
with the healing earth.
God of our winter changing, bless your people
with a new season.
God of our winter experience, bless your
people with a clear vision.

THE BLESSING OF EUCHARIST

*I am the bread of life. Whoever comes to
me will never be hungry and whoever
believes in me shall never be thirsty.*

John 6

Eucharist Thoughts

There was a famine in the land and a culture
of enterprise was choking from waste
products that stopped the flow of the river.
Despite the food mountains the people
continued to kill the robins and the children
were starved in the studios of pornographic
wealth. The absence of food was evident
everywhere. The death of life was disguised in
the rise of empires and in the distortion of
language. It was a young Jewish man who first
identified the problem as a failure to taste life.
He moved the life debate beyond the
mechanics of breathing, paying taxes and
carrying water and he spoke of truth, of light

and of destiny. He spoke of Eucharist, in the field, on the mountain side and in the city and the cosmic character of this new energy began to move the earth. The Passover table became the gathering place, an altar for the world. As the people came to share the meal they heard the choirs of angels and they saw the meeting of heaven and earth and every tribe and tongue was embraced and restored in the blood of the Lamb. It was the holy hour, the hour of love's great triumph. He, who had been with God in the beginning, was now standing at the source, pouring out the river over the plains, across the continents, into history. He was making all time, God's time, one time. This was the genetic link, the great connection, the communion for which all creation yearns. At the table in Jerusalem he restored the purpose to time and space; he opened God's capacity on the world. The human senses began to open and the bread and wine became the meeting place for all who hunger and thirst.

O Lamb of God, you danced in our meadows;
bless the hands of your people with giving and
receiving.

O Lamb of God, you offered yourself to set us
free; bless our speaking with the language of
love.

O Lamb of God, you changed the bread and
wine; bless our attitudes with thoughts of
conversion.

O Lamb of God, you fulfilled the ancient
covenant; bless our promises with faithful
journeys.

O Lamb of God, you gave the gift of your life;
bless our loving with the holiness of sacrifice.

O Lamb of God, you left food for the world;
bless our generosity with shared moments.

O Lamb of God, you called us to communion;
bless our relationships with compassion and
forgiveness.

O Lamb of God, you stayed with us across the
years; bless our longings with communion.

Words of Blessing

For the Victory

Blessed be God.
Blessed be the Victory of God over death.
Blessed be the Victory of God who makes all
things new.
Blessed be the Tenderness of God who will
wipe every tear from our eyes.
Blessed be the Healing of God who will end
all mourning and pain.
Blessed be the Word of God that is sure and
true.
Blessed be the Dwelling of God who has
pitched his tent with his people.
Blessed be the Timelessness of God, the Alpha
and the Omega.
Blessed be the Faithfulness of God, the
Beginning and the End.
Blessed be the Lamb of God who sits on the
throne of God.
Blessed be the Lamb of God who now stands
where the Temple stood.
Blessed be the Lamb of God, the river of life
gushing from the throne.

Blessed be the Lamb of God who gives fruit to heal the nations.
Blessed be the Lamb of God who has ended the grip of night.
Blessed be the Lamb of God who lights the city with his lamp.
Blessed be the Woman of God, clothed with the sun, standing on the moon.
Blessed be the Angels of God who sing God's praises.
Blessed be the City of God, coming down out of heaven.
Blessed be the Works of God, great and marvellous in their splendour.
Blessed be the New Jerusalem, precious jewel of God's achievement.
Blessed be God who lives forever.
Praise, glory, wisdom, thanks, honour, power and strength to our God forever and ever.
Amen.

Revelation 21:1-6